A Plant Has Needs

by Cynthia Swain

I need to know these words.

air

food

light

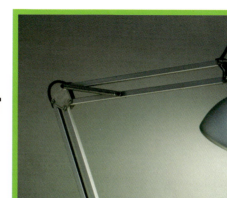

water

This plant has **water**.

This plant has rain.

This plant has sun.

This plant has **light**.

This plant has **air**.

This plant has **food**.

This plant has soil.